HOMEWORK HELPERS

Times Tables for School

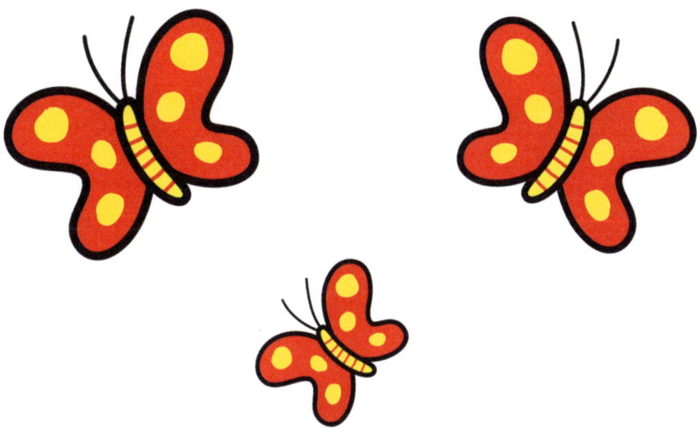

Illustrated by Ian Cunliffe

1 Read the times tables list aloud.

Try to remember the answers.

6 Times Table

0 x 6 = 0

1 x 6 = 6

2 x 6 = 12

3 x 6 = 18

4 x 6 = 24

5 x 6 = 30

6 x 6 = 36

7 x 6 = 42

8 x 6 = 48

9 x 6 = 54

10 x 6 = 60

11 x 6 = 66

12 x 6 = 72

2 What things can you find in the picture to count?

3 Look at the number words and what they mean. What do you notice about each word?

6 – six 6th – sixth

Word	Meaning
sextuple	six times as much
hexagon	a flat shape with six equal sides
sextuplets	six children born at the same time
sextet	six singers or musicians

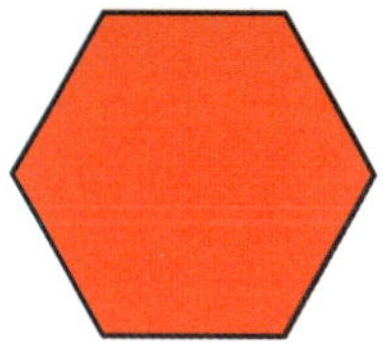

1	2	3	4	5	6	7	8	9	10
11	12	13	14	15	16	17	18	19	20
21	22	23	24	25	26	27	28	29	30
31	32	33	34	35	36	37	38	39	40
41	42	43	44	45	46	47	48	49	50
51	52	53	54	55	56	57	58	59	60
61	62	63	64	65	66	67	68	69	70
71	72	73	74	75	76	77	78	79	80
81	82	83	84	85	86	87	88	89	90
91	92	93	94	95	96	97	98	99	100

The numbers in green show the six times table. What is the pattern of the numbers in the green squares?

4 What pattern can you see on the number grid?

Contents

1 Times Table

0 x 1 = 0

1 x 1 = 1

2 x 1 = 2

3 x 1 = 3

4 x 1 = 4

5 x 1 = 5

6 x 1 = 6

7 x 1 = 7

8 x 1 = 8

9 x 1 = 9

10 x 1 = 10

11 x 1 = 11

12 x 1 = 12

1 – one   1st – first

Word	Meaning
single	one, on its own
unicycle	one-wheeled cycle
solo	for one person
once	one time

1	2	3	4	5	6	7	8	9	10
11	12	13	14	15	16	17	18	19	20
21	22	23	24	25	26	27	28	29	30
31	32	33	34	35	36	37	38	39	40
41	42	43	44	45	46	47	48	49	50
51	52	53	54	55	56	57	58	59	60
61	62	63	64	65	66	67	68	69	70
71	72	73	74	75	76	77	78	79	80
81	82	83	84	85	86	87	88	89	90
91	92	93	94	95	96	97	98	99	100

Here are the numbers from one to one hundred in a number grid. This shows the one times table.

2 Times Table

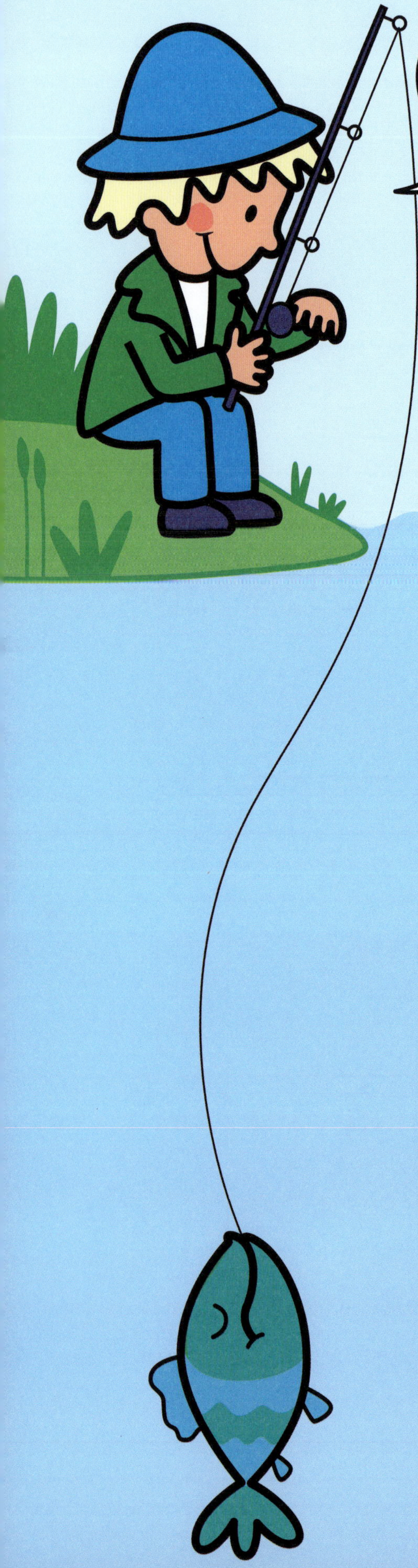

0 x 2 = 0

1 x 2 = 2

2 x 2 = 4

3 x 2 = 6

4 x 2 = 8

5 x 2 = 10

6 x 2 = 12

7 x 2 = 14

8 x 2 = 16

9 x 2 = 18

10 x 2 = 20

11 x 2 = 22

12 x 2 = 24

2 – two   2nd – second

Word	**Meaning**
double	two times as much
pair	two matching items
bicycle	two-wheeled cycle
twice	two times
twins	two children born at the same time

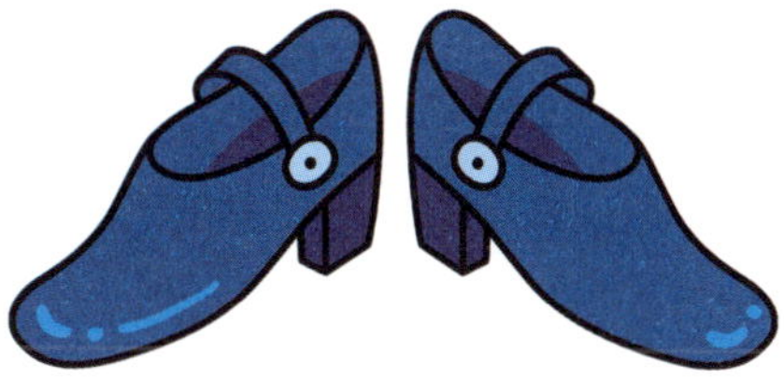

1	2	3	4	5	6	7	8	9	10
11	12	13	14	15	16	17	18	19	20
21	22	23	24	25	26	27	28	29	30
31	32	33	34	35	36	37	38	39	40
41	42	43	44	45	46	47	48	49	50
51	52	53	54	55	56	57	58	59	60
61	62	63	64	65	66	67	68	69	70
71	72	73	74	75	76	77	78	79	80
81	82	83	84	85	86	87	88	89	90
91	92	93	94	95	96	97	98	99	100

The numbers in blue show the pattern of the two times table. What do you notice about the numbers in the blue columns?

3 Times Table

How many mice are eating cheese?

0 x 3 = 0

1 x 3 = 3

2 x 3 = 6

3 x 3 = 9

4 x 3 = 12

5 x 3 = 15

6 x 3 = 18

7 x 3 = 21

8 x 3 = 24

9 x 3 = 27

10 x 3 = 30

11 x 3 = 33

12 x 3 = 36

3 – three 3rd – third

Word	**Meaning**
triple, treble	three times as much
tricycle	three-wheeled cycle
triangle	three-sided flat shape
trilogy	three part book, play or film
triplets	three children born at the same time

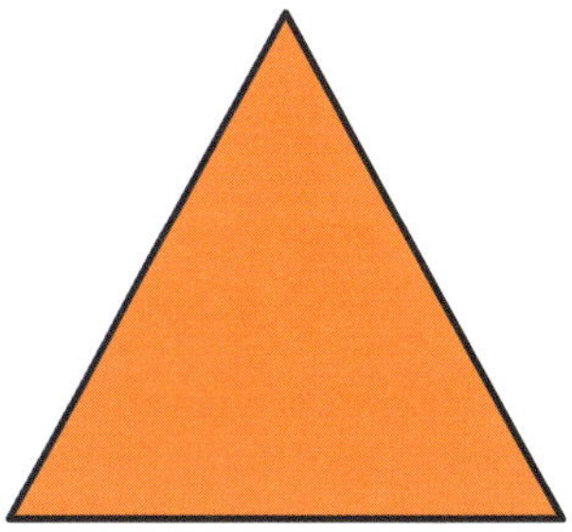

1	2	3	4	5	6	7	8	9	10
11	12	13	14	15	16	17	18	19	20
21	22	23	24	25	26	27	28	29	30
31	32	33	34	35	36	37	38	39	40
41	42	43	44	45	46	47	48	49	50
51	52	53	54	55	56	57	58	59	60
61	62	63	64	65	66	67	68	69	70
71	72	73	74	75	76	77	78	79	80
81	82	83	84	85	86	87	88	89	90
91	92	93	94	95	96	97	98	99	100

The numbers in red show the pattern of the three times table. What do you notice about the red numbers going downwards?

4 Times Table

0 x 4 = 0

1 x 4 = 4

2 x 4 = 8

3 x 4 = 12

4 x 4 = 16

5 x 4 = 20

6 x 4 = 24

7 x 4 = 28

8 x 4 = 32

9 x 4 = 36

10 x 4 = 40

11 x 4 = 44

12 x 4 = 48

4 – four 4th – fourth

Word	**Meaning**
quadruple	four times as much
quarter	one of four equal parts of a whole
square	a flat shape with four equal sides
quadruplets	four children born at the same time

1	2	3	4	5	6	7	8	9	10
11	12	13	14	15	16	17	18	19	20
21	22	23	24	25	26	27	28	29	30
31	32	33	34	35	36	37	38	39	40
41	42	43	44	45	46	47	48	49	50
51	52	53	54	55	56	57	58	59	60
61	62	63	64	65	66	67	68	69	70
71	72	73	74	75	76	77	78	79	80
81	82	83	84	85	86	87	88	89	90
91	92	93	94	95	96	97	98	99	100

The numbers in orange show the four times table.
What do you notice about it?
Does it remind you of the two times table?

5 Times Table

0 x 5 = 0

1 x 5 = 5

2 x 5 = 10

3 x 5 = 15

4 x 5 = 20

5 x 5 = 25

6 x 5 = 30

7 x 5 = 35

8 x 5 = 40

9 x 5 = 45

10 x 5 = 50

11 x 5 = 55

12 x 5 = 60

5 – five 5th – fifth

Word	**Meaning**
quintuple	five times as much
pentagon	a shape with five sides
quintet	five singers or musicians
pentathlon	an athletics contest with five events

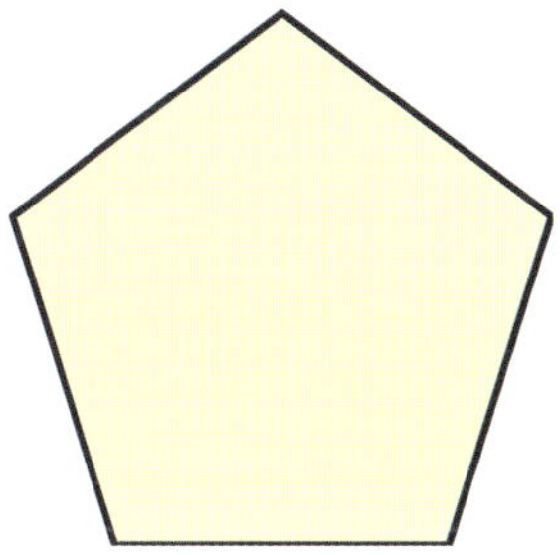

1	2	3	4	5	6	7	8	9	10
11	12	13	14	15	16	17	18	19	20
21	22	23	24	25	26	27	28	29	30
31	32	33	34	35	36	37	38	39	40
41	42	43	44	45	46	47	48	49	50
51	52	53	54	55	56	57	58	59	60
61	62	63	64	65	66	67	68	69	70
71	72	73	74	75	76	77	78	79	80
81	82	83	84	85	86	87	88	89	90
91	92	93	94	95	96	97	98	99	100

The numbers in yellow show the five times table. Look at the yellow columns. Do you notice anything about the units?

6 Times Table

0 x 6 = 0

1 x 6 = 6

2 x 6 = 12

3 x 6 = 18

4 x 6 = 24

5 x 6 = 30

6 x 6 = 36

7 x 6 = 42

8 x 6 = 48

9 x 6 = 54

10 x 6 = 60

11 x 6 = 66

12 x 6 = 72

6 – six   6th – sixth

Word	**Meaning**
sextuple	six times as much
hexagon	a flat shape with six equal sides
sextuplets	six children born at the same time
sextet	six singers or musicians

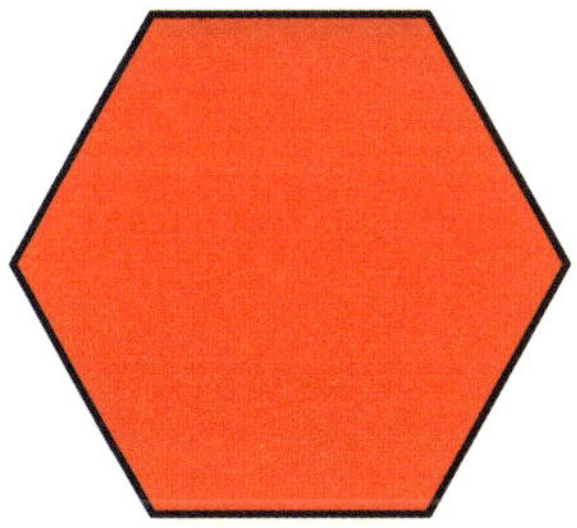

1	2	3	4	5	6	7	8	9	10
11	12	13	14	15	16	17	18	19	20
21	22	23	24	25	26	27	28	29	30
31	32	33	34	35	36	37	38	39	40
41	42	43	44	45	46	47	48	49	50
51	52	53	54	55	56	57	58	59	60
61	62	63	64	65	66	67	68	69	70
71	72	73	74	75	76	77	78	79	80
81	82	83	84	85	86	87	88	89	90
91	92	93	94	95	96	97	98	99	100

The numbers in green show the six times table. What is the pattern of the numbers in the green squares?

7 Times Table

0 x 7 = 0

1 x 7 = 7

2 x 7 = 14

3 x 7 = 21

4 x 7 = 28

5 x 7 = 35

6 x 7 = 42

7 x 7 = 49

8 x 7 = 56

9 x 7 = 63

10 x 7 = 70

11 x 7 = 77

12 x 7 = 84

7 – seven   7th – seventh

Word	**Meaning**
September	in Roman times, this was the seventh month of the year
septennial	lasting for seven years
heptagon	a seven-sided flat shape
septet	seven singers or musicians

1	2	3	4	5	6	7	8	9	10
11	12	13	14	15	16	17	18	19	20
21	22	23	24	25	26	27	28	29	30
31	32	33	34	35	36	37	38	39	40
41	42	43	44	45	46	47	48	49	50
51	52	53	54	55	56	57	58	59	60
61	62	63	64	65	66	67	68	69	70
71	72	73	74	75	76	77	78	79	80
81	82	83	84	85	86	87	88	89	90
91	92	93	94	95	96	97	98	99	100

The numbers in yellow show the pattern of the seven times table. What do you notice this time?

8 Times Table

0 x 8 = 0
1 x 8 = 8
2 x 8 = 16
3 x 8 = 24
4 x 8 = 32
5 x 8 = 40
6 x 8 = 48
7 x 8 = 56
8 x 8 = 64
9 x 8 = 72
10 x 8 = 80
11 x 8 = 88
12 x 8 = 96

8 – eight 8th – eighth

Word	Meaning
October	in Roman times, this was the eighth month of the year
octagon	an eight-sided flat shape
octopus	a sea creature with eight tentacles
octet	eight singers or musicians

1	2	3	4	5	6	7	8	9	10
11	12	13	14	15	16	17	18	19	20
21	22	23	24	25	26	27	28	29	30
31	32	33	34	35	36	37	38	39	40
41	42	43	44	45	46	47	48	49	50
51	52	53	54	55	56	57	58	59	60
61	62	63	64	65	66	67	68	69	70
71	72	73	74	75	76	77	78	79	80
81	82	83	84	85	86	87	88	89	90
91	92	93	94	95	96	97	98	99	100

The numbers in blue show the pattern of the eight times table. Can you see a pattern in the numbers below the blue squares?

9 Times Table

0 x 9 =	0
1 x 9 =	9
2 x 9 =	18
3 x 9 =	27
4 x 9 =	36
5 x 9 =	45
6 x 9 =	54
7 x 9 =	63
8 x 9 =	72
9 x 9 =	81
10 x 9 =	90
11 x 9 =	99
12 x 9 =	108

9 – nine 9th – ninth

Word	**Meaning**
November	in Roman times, this was the ninth month of the year
nonagon	nine-sided flat shape
nonet	nine singers or musicians

1	2	3	4	5	6	7	8	9	10
11	12	13	14	15	16	17	18	19	20
21	22	23	24	25	26	27	28	29	30
31	32	33	34	35	36	37	38	39	40
41	42	43	44	45	46	47	48	49	50
51	52	53	54	55	56	57	58	59	60
61	62	63	64	65	66	67	68	69	70
71	72	73	74	75	76	77	78	79	80
81	82	83	84	85	86	87	88	89	90
91	92	93	94	95	96	97	98	99	100

The numbers in pink show the pattern of the nine times table. What is the pattern of the tens? What is the pattern of the units?

10 Times Table

0	x	10	=	0
1	x	10	=	10
2	x	10	=	20
3	x	10	=	30
4	x	10	=	40
5	x	10	=	50
6	x	10	=	60
7	x	10	=	70
8	x	10	=	80
9	x	10	=	90
10	x	10	=	100
11	x	10	=	110
12	x	10	=	120

10 – ten 10th – tenth

Word	**Meaning**
December	in Roman times, this was the tenth month
decade	ten years
decagon	ten-sided shape
decathlon	an athletic contest with ten events

1	2	3	4	5	6	7	8	9	10
11	12	13	14	15	16	17	18	19	20
21	22	23	24	25	26	27	28	29	30
31	32	33	34	35	36	37	38	39	40
41	42	43	44	45	46	47	48	49	50
51	52	53	54	55	56	57	58	59	60
61	62	63	64	65	66	67	68	69	70
71	72	73	74	75	76	77	78	79	80
81	82	83	84	85	86	87	88	89	90
91	92	93	94	95	96	97	98	99	100

The numbers in blue show the ten times table.
What is the pattern of the tens?
What is the pattern of the units?

11 Times Table

0 x 11 = 0

1 x 11 = 11

2 x 11 = 22

3 x 11 = 33

4 x 11 = 44

5 x 11 = 55

6 x 11 = 66

7 x 11 = 77

8 x 11 = 88

9 x 11 = 99

10 x 11 = 110

11 x 11 = 121

12 x 11 = 132

11 – eleven 11th – eleventh

Word	**Meaning**
hendecagon	eleven-sided flat shape

1	2	3	4	5	6	7	8	9	10
11	12	13	14	15	16	17	18	19	20
21	22	23	24	25	26	27	28	29	30
31	32	33	34	35	36	37	38	39	40
41	42	43	44	45	46	47	48	49	50
51	52	53	54	55	56	57	58	59	60
61	62	63	64	65	66	67	68	69	70
71	72	73	74	75	76	77	78	79	80
81	82	83	84	85	86	87	88	89	90
91	92	93	94	95	96	97	98	99	100

The numbers in green show the eleven times table.
What do you notice about the tens and units?
Can you see a link with the one times table?

12 Times Table

0 x 12 = 0

1 x 12 = 12

2 x 12 = 24

3 x 12 = 36

4 x 12 = 48

5 x 12 = 60

6 x 12 = 72

7 x 12 = 84

8 x 12 = 96

9 x 12 = 108

10 x 12 = 120

11 x 12 = 132

12 x 12 = 144

12 – twelve 12th – twelfth

Word	**Meaning**
dodecagon	twelve-sided flat shape
dozen	twelve of something

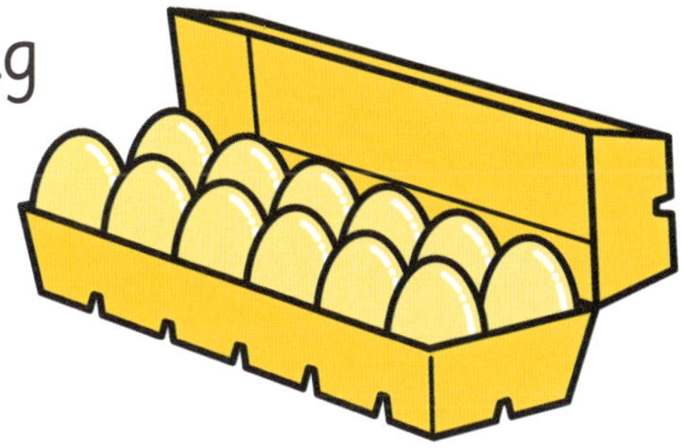

1	2	3	4	5	6	7	8	9	10
11	12	13	14	15	16	17	18	19	20
21	22	23	24	25	26	27	28	29	30
31	32	33	34	35	36	37	38	39	40
41	42	43	44	45	46	47	48	49	50
51	52	53	54	55	56	57	58	59	60
61	62	63	64	65	66	67	68	69	70
71	72	73	74	75	76	77	78	79	80
81	82	83	84	85	86	87	88	89	90
91	92	93	94	95	96	97	98	99	100

The numbers in purple show the twelve times table.
What is the pattern of the numbers this time?

1 Times Table

0 x 1 = 0
1 x 1 = 1
2 x 1 = 2
3 x 1 = 3
4 x 1 = 4
5 x 1 = 5
6 x 1 = 6
7 x 1 = 7
8 x 1 = 8
9 x 1 = 9
10 x 1 = 10
11 x 1 = 11
12 x 1 = 12

2 Times Table

0 x 2 = 0
1 x 2 = 2
2 x 2 = 4
3 x 2 = 6
4 x 2 = 8
5 x 2 = 10
6 x 2 = 12
7 x 2 = 14
8 x 2 = 16
9 x 2 = 18
10 x 2 = 20
11 x 2 = 22
12 x 2 = 24

3 Times Table

0 x 3 = 0
1 x 3 = 3
2 x 3 = 6
3 x 3 = 9
4 x 3 = 12
5 x 3 = 15
6 x 3 = 18
7 x 3 = 21
8 x 3 = 24
9 x 3 = 27
10 x 3 = 30
11 x 3 = 33
12 x 3 = 36

7 Times Table

0 x 7 = 0
1 x 7 = 7
2 x 7 = 14
3 x 7 = 21
4 x 7 = 28
5 x 7 = 35
6 x 7 = 42
7 x 7 = 49
8 x 7 = 56
9 x 7 = 63
10 x 7 = 70
11 x 7 = 77
12 x 7 = 84

8 Times Table

0 x 8 = 0
1 x 8 = 8
2 x 8 = 16
3 x 8 = 24
4 x 8 = 32
5 x 8 = 40
6 x 8 = 48
7 x 8 = 56
8 x 8 = 64
9 x 8 = 72
10 x 8 = 80
11 x 8 = 88
12 x 8 = 96

9 Times Table

0 x 9 = 0
1 x 9 = 9
2 x 9 = 18
3 x 9 = 27
4 x 9 = 36
5 x 9 = 45
6 x 9 = 54
7 x 9 = 63
8 x 9 = 72
9 x 9 = 81
10 x 9 = 90
11 x 9 = 99
12 x 9 = 108

4 Times Table

0 x 4 = 0
1 x 4 = 4
2 x 4 = 8
3 x 4 = 12
4 x 4 = 16
5 x 4 = 20
6 x 4 = 24
7 x 4 = 28
8 x 4 = 32
9 x 4 = 36
10 x 4 = 40
11 x 4 = 44
12 x 4 = 48

5 Times Table

0 x 5 = 0
1 x 5 = 5
2 x 5 = 10
3 x 5 = 15
4 x 5 = 20
5 x 5 = 25
6 x 5 = 30
7 x 5 = 35
8 x 5 = 40
9 x 5 = 45
10 x 5 = 50
11 x 5 = 55
12 x 5 = 60

6 Times Table

0 x 6 = 0
1 x 6 = 6
2 x 6 = 12
3 x 6 = 18
4 x 6 = 24
5 x 6 = 30
6 x 6 = 36
7 x 6 = 42
8 x 6 = 48
9 x 6 = 54
10 x 6 = 60
11 x 6 = 66
12 x 6 = 72

10 Times Table

0 x 10 = 0
1 x 10 = 10
2 x 10 = 20
3 x 10 = 30
4 x 10 = 40
5 x 10 = 50
6 x 10 = 60
7 x 10 = 70
8 x 10 = 80
9 x 10 = 90
10 x 10 = 100
11 x 10 = 110
12 x 10 = 120

11 Times Table

0 x 11 = 0
1 x 11 = 11
2 x 11 = 22
3 x 11 = 33
4 x 11 = 44
5 x 11 = 55
6 x 11 = 66
7 x 11 = 77
8 x 11 = 88
9 x 11 = 99
10 x 11 = 110
11 x 11 = 121
12 x 11 = 132

12 Times Table

0 x 12 = 0
1 x 12 = 12
2 x 12 = 24
3 x 12 = 36
4 x 12 = 48
5 x 12 = 60
6 x 12 = 72
7 x 12 = 84
8 x 12 = 96
9 x 12 = 108
10 x 12 = 120
11 x 12 = 132
12 x 12 = 144

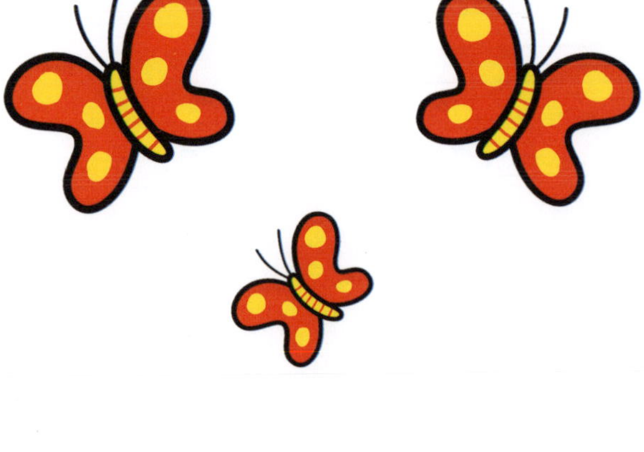